ULTIMATE **KILLERS**

First published 2001 by Boxtree, an imprint of
Macmillan Publishers Ltd, 25 Eccleston Place,
London, SW1W 9NF; Basingstoke and Oxford
Associated companies throughout the world

www.macmillan.co.uk

ISBN 0 7522 1889 1

Text copyright © Steve Leonard 2001
Animal fact boxes by Victoria Webb

The right of Steve Leonard to be identified as the
author of this work has been asserted by him in
accordance with the Copyright, Designs and
Patents Act 1988.

By arrangement with the BBC

The BBC logo is a trademark of the British
Broadcasting Corporation and is used under
licence.

BBC logo © BBC 1996

9 8 7 6 5 4 3 2 1

A CIP catalogue record for this book is available
from the British Library.

Inside design by Dan Newman@Perfect Bound
Colour reproduction by Aylesbury Studios
Printed in the E.C.

All photographs copyright © Steve Leonard
except: page 16, supplied by BBC Natural History
Unit © Michael Pitts; page 21, supplied by NHPA ©
Norbert Wu; page 34, © Leo Dickinson; page 73,
supplied by NHPA © Anthony Bannister; page 85,
suppled by NHPA © A.N.T; page 118, supplied by
BBC Natural History Unit © Lawrence Michael.

ULTIMATE KILLERS

A Quest for The World's Deadliest Animal

STEVE LEONARD

BOXTREE

contents

foreword

The quest to find the world's Ultimate Killers began a long time ago. It started with just an idea. Then came the difficult bit – the research. The *Ultimate Killers* team spent months sitting in a cramped basement office, slogging away on the Internet and on the phone, putting together ideas for the programme. I was the lucky one. I got to go out and experience all the adventures they had planned, along with my trusty companions Simon Wagen (cameraman) and Jake Drake-Brockman (soundman).

And what an experience it was. I spent an entire year filming for this series, travelling all over the planet, to five out of six of the continents. In all I visited fourteen different countries with huge variations in climates and conditions; from the High Arctic, where the sun never set and temperatures dropped to –25 degrees centigrade, to the deserts of Namibia, where the sun beat down relentlessly.

Sometimes the sequences came easily. The animals simply turned up and behaved well. At other times we had to work much harder, trekking through jungles, driving for miles on snowmobiles or waiting days for a break in the weather. Even when we got all the other things right, often the animals had the cheek not to perform for the camera or even to turn up at all. Mostly, though, we were very lucky, catching animal behaviour rarely seen on camera and getting in really close to the action.

I am sometimes surprised that I am still in one piece. I have jumped out of a balloon at 10,000 feet, swum with sharks, been chased by a cheetah and held the most venomous animal in the world in my hands. And that was just before lunch. Thankfully, I was privileged to meet and work alongside some very dedicated and knowledgeable people. All the contributors who helped me get close to the action showed a great deal of enthusiasm about their species and a great deal of patience with me.

This book, like the series, is split into categories: Speed, Venom, Defenders, Strength, Pack Hunters, and Man-Eaters. Some of you will find a few surprises in these categories: animals you never expected to be included and some you thought should have been but were not. There are so many impressive animals out there that we could not hope to include them all.

Looking back over all that I have done for this series, I cannot believe I managed to fit all these once-in-a-lifetime experiences into one year. I hope you enjoy reading about them, because, believe me, it was an absolute blast doing it.

Steve Leonard

speed

The mantis shrimp is reputed to be the fastest animal on the planet. It can impale passing fish in about 3 milliseconds. But it doesn't pursue its prey – it sits and waits – and what I am interested in is the chase, not the kill. Maybe this chapter should have been called 'Pursuit'.

Put yourself in the position of potential prey. You are grazing away peacefully, when you spot something moving in the bushes. A glimpse of spotted fur through the branches. A long striped tail flicking excitedly. A horrible feeling settles as adrenaline pumps through your bloodstream readying you for flight. You have a good head start, but deep down you know that isn't good enough. For the briefest of moments, you both freeze and lock eyes.

Then – boom – you're off, racing across the plains. For the first few seconds you think you just might make it – but you can feel its presence behind you, gaining, always gaining. You chance a look behind and see it lunge at your legs. No matter how hard you push it will always have that edge. So with your lungs roaring and heart fit to burst you race on until your legs are knocked sideways and you crash to the ground. You're nailed.

Being faster than the animal you want to catch comes at a cost. Weight and strength have to be sacrificed to gain those few extra miles an hour and that can leave you vulnerable to attack or injury. Injury can be as good as death because if the predator can't move at speed the advantage is gone and the prey escapes.

Most people assume that the fastest animal in the world is the cheetah. It is the fastest land animal, but there is a lot more to the planet than land. There were a few surprises in this category for me, and I think there will be for you too.

cheetah

Everybody knows the cheetah is the fastest land animal, but where do you go to see one in action? The best place for us was in Okanjima, Namibia, home to Africat. Africat is a charity set up for the protection of the big cats, mainly cheetahs and leopards, but increasingly including other large African carnivores. A lot of the cheetahs are rescued from farmland where they would otherwise be shot, and housed until they can be relocated. There are also a small number of orphaned cheetahs that are too tame to release and these are kept for education and tourism.

To see the cheetahs in action we went to a greyhound-training lure that had been set up on a sandy airstrip. The lure is basically a scrap of cloth attached to a rope that is dragged along the ground by an electric motor. All we needed now was a cheetah.

Nandi, an adult female cheetah, arrived in a Land-Rover with Carla Conradie, who cares for the cheetahs here. Cheetahs are beautiful creatures and everybody crowded round to get a close look. The sound of a cheetah purring is incredible, as you don't expect to hear that sound from such a large animal.

Dave is an English cameraman who moved his home to Africat after coming here for the first time five years ago. He now works as a volunteer here in between filming trips and operated the lure for us.

When we were ready Nandi was let out of the vehicle and Dave set the lure running. She focused straight away on the movement of the lure. The first few times round she lunged at it and caught it almost immediately. Jake had a laser speed gun, as used by traffic police, and clocked her at 28 miles an hour – she didn't even look like she had broken out of a trot. Sprinting flat out, I could only manage 16 miles per hour.

After a few times round, Nandi gave up and lay down. It was obvious that she was bored. She wasn't tired or panting yet and it seemed more as though she was telling us 'This is too easy.'

Carla told us we could approach Nandi and pet her. Jake and I took her up on the offer and went to make friends. She was quiet for about five seconds and then rounded on Jake. Before he could retreat she had both dew-claws sunk into his leg and was trying to bite him. Dave rushed in and we managed to get her off him. This was very unusual behaviour for Nandi. In fact, she had only ever attacked one other person, but he looked similar to Jake in build and hair colour. Jake wasn't too shook up and we washed down his wounds. I took great relish in spraying a stinging antiseptic on his legs as he hopped about. He had quite a number of claw marks on his leg, but none was that deep.

Even when we were finished cleaning him up, Nandi was still eyeing him up from a distance and Dave had to keep her away.

The main piece of filming was me being chased by one of the cheetahs and after what happened to Jake, I was less than confident about my chances of escaping unscathed.

Opposite: With fairly poor stamina, cheetahs do not expend any more energy than is strictly necessary.

The cheetah can reach 60mph for short distances, and has a stride length of 23 feet

Thankfully the cheetah we were using for this was Tarka, who was another orphan cheetah, but a young playful male. The idea was that I would start running and he would try and catch me. To give me a chance I had about a 30-yard head start on Tarka. I didn't know whether he would leap on my back or sink his claws into my legs. It was good motivation to sprint as fast as I could, though.

I thought I would at least get halfway to the camera before Tarka caught me, but without even trying he was right behind me after a matter of seconds. Thankfully

he only batted my legs gently with his forepaws. It kind of tickled and made running difficult but at least there was no blood.

Tarka bored very quickly and we had to entice him with as many toys as possible, from a basketball to a stuffed toy called 'Mr Penguin'. Mr Penguin had taken a fair battering over the months Tarka has been here and was unrecognizable as a bird to us, but Tarka did show some fleeting interest when it made an appearance.

One thing Tarka really liked was attacking Jake. There is something about that

Right: The acceleration of a pickup is no match for the cheetah which can do 0–60mph in about 3–4 seconds.

man that cheetahs either dislike or find appetising. He is quite small and furry, so maybe that's it. On a number of occasions Tarka leapt on Jake's back and tried to bite him. He now has a hole in a T-shirt with a good story behind it.

I ran back and forth with all manner of interesting toys, but to no avail. Carla suggested hanging some meat off my belt and Marielle, the director, thought this was a promising idea. Not surprisingly, I wasn't as keen on the idea, and thankfully it was never put into action. Anyway, a cheetah chasing me was no real challenge.

It was time to bring back Nandi. Jake was feeling a little nervous after their previous introduction, but thankfully she seemed to have forgotten him for the moment. After working with Tarka, who isn't fully grown, it was amazing to see Nandi again. She was much more muscular

Opposite: Unlike other large cats cheetahs are relatively easy to tame.

than the younger male and therefore seemed far more intimidating. In fact, her behaviour was as bad as her apparent image. As soon as she was out of the vehicle she grabbed everything she could get her teeth into. She loved fleeces and fluffy things, so a few more items of clothing now have cheetah holes in them.

She leapt onto the pickup truck roof and Jake at one point had to fend her off with Simon's camera. I was getting more confident around the cheetahs in general, so I could help get her off things she shouldn't be playing with. At one point Dave and I had to open her jaws with our hands to stop her from biting through the sound cables.

Once we got set up, Nandi was instantly interested in the meaty bone we had acquired as a bait, so much so that she kept trying to leap back onto the pickup before we even set off. Dave finally got us underway and I threw the bone out, attached to a rope. She was on it in an instant. Dave accelerated hard, but not enough to beat Nandi. She pounced on the meat and I thought I was going to lose it. I managed to yank it free and Dave kept us going. I was reeling in the rope and Dave was pushing the pedal hard but still Nandi was gaining. We got to over 40 miles per hour and she was still with us. It was an awesome sight to see her at full gallop, stretching that long spine. Her legs were moving so fast that it seemed as though she was floating. At full speed a cheetah has a stride length of up to 23 feet.

Now I fully appreciate how feeble a sprinter I am compared to Nandi. All that acceleration comes at a cost, however, as she was thoroughly pooped after only two runs and wouldn't run again that day. We thanked her by letting her take the bone she had run for. She wandered off into the bush to get her breath back before enjoying her treat.

CHEETAH (acinonyx jubatus)

The cheetah is the fastest land animal over short distances, reaching speeds of 60mph (96km/h). The long, fluid body is streamlined, like that of a greyhound and a flexible spine acts like a spring for the powerful back legs, giving about 30in (75cm) added reach for each step. Claws and special pads on the feet provide good grip, the tail acts as a rudder for quick turning and large nostrils allow a large intake of air. Cheetahs can only maintain top speed for about 300yd (274m) as the spring-like movement is very taxing. They take small antelope, such as springbok, steenbok, impala and gazelle, and the young of larger animals, including kudu, hartebeest, oryx, roan and sable. The biggest populations of cheetah live in Namibia; smaller populations occur in Botswana, Zimbabwe, South Africa, Kenya and Tanzania, while nineteen other countries have even fewer. Cheetah habitat includes open grasslands, savannah, woodlands and bush country; they need bushes and tall grass to enable them to hide from other predators. Cheetahs stand about 32in (81cm) tall at the shoulder, weigh 71–141lb (36–64kg) and from nose to tail are 76–88in (1.9–2.2m) long. They can live for about twelve years in the wild.

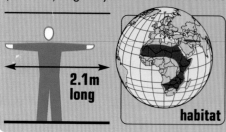

2.1m long

habitat

top speed

barracuda

Nobody knows more about barracuda behaviour than Captain Slate. He owns a diving centre in Key Largo, Florida, and has been feeding barracuda on the reefs here for twenty-eight years. His speciality is to place fish in his mouth and let the barracuda zoom in and take the bait from his lips. We set out in one of his boats to go and see this at first hand.

The barracuda are quick and accurate but occasionally things go a little wrong. Captain Slate showed me the numerous scars on his hands from bites. The worst bite to his hand narrowly missed his tendons and required twenty-five stitches.

More impressive even than his scar collection is the damage that the barracuda have done to some of Captain Slate's kit. He showed me an air hose from his scuba kit that a barracuda bit right through. It was

good thick rubber and had had been cut cleaner than with a knife. He now carries a spare air supply in case this happens again.

The scariest thing he had in his collection was his mask, which a barracuda had ripped off. He thought it had just knocked it off his face, but when he tried to put it back on he noticed that the whole side had been bitten right through. He was millimetres away from needing reconstructive facial surgery or losing an eye. The last thing to have bitten him, however, was a moray eel, for which he was going to require surgery.

Because of his impending operation, Captain Slate couldn't dive, so one of his crew, Brian, was coming down with us to feed the barracuda. Captain Slate had a few words of warning for me before I left the boat. The main thing was to keep my hands close to my body when Brian was feeding, as otherwise I ran the risk of losing a finger or two to a barracuda.

The reef bottom was only about 30 feet down, so it was very light and warm. We settled onto a patch of sand and Brian dug out a few bait-fish to draw the barracuda. Initially the only thing we drew were a shoal of lovely yellow fish. The next fish to turn up were two very cheeky nurse sharks. They made numerous attempts to get inside the bait bag. Brian was scratching their heads and they seemed unperturbed, so I reached out for quick feel. Their skin is quite abrasive, like fine sandpaper. It was magical to be able to run my hands along their flanks without scaring them off.

We were still on the lookout for a barracuda when we had another visitor. A

Opposite: Every inch of the barracuda's torpedo-shaped body is designed for speed.
Below: Barracudas have played havoc with Captain Slate's equipment – and hands.

Above: When swimming with the barracuda, I managed to avoid injury.

green moray eel came swimming over looking for a free meal. It had no fear of us at all. Brian stroked its body as it wound its way around him. Seeing its dangerous-looking mouth, I decided to keep my hands to myself. I felt it pass between my legs and it appeared up in front of me. I couldn't resist reaching out to caress it as it slipped by. It felt like super-soft velvet slipping between my hands.

I was still enthralled with the moray when I felt Brian nudge me. He was pointing out two barracuda that were coasting around above us. I had never seen them underwater before and never this big. These two were about 30 inches in length, and were very impressive-looking fish. Barracuda are not built for looks, just pure speed. They have torpedo-shaped

bodies fronted by a set of intimidating jaws complete with massive sharp teeth. Most fish swallow their food whole, whereas barracuda, like sharks, have the ability to bite through their prey before swallowing it.

They cruised around us, knowing from experience that a meal was going to be on offer. Brian slipped a fish from the bait bag and concealed it in his hands. This bit was crucial, because if the barracuda spotted it Brian would need stitches in his hand within a blink of an eye. When he thought one of the barracuda was lined up properly he took his regulator from his mouth and held the fish between his lips. The barracuda zipped in and snatched it away.

I was a little disappointed that it didn't burst into full speed, but these fish have learned that they don't need to. It did give

GREAT BARRACUDA (sphyraena barracuda)

There are eighteen species of barracuda, the largest of which is the great barracuda. Adult barracuda reach lengths of 3.3–4.9ft (1–1.5m). Great barracuda are found in most tropical and subtropical habitats and are found in greatest numbers in the Western Atlantic from Florida to Venezuela, including the Caribbean Sea and Gulf of Mexico. They are generally found in areas of coral reef, seagrass and mangrove habitat. Barracuda are voracious hunters, feeding during the day on many species of fish as well as seabirds. Their torpedo-shaped body allows them to approach prey slowly and silently. Once prey is in range, the barracuda uses its incredible acceleration – 0–45mph (0–72km/h) in 0.75 seconds – to dart forward and grab the prey before it can react. Barracuda have sharp, jagged teeth, and strong tearing jaws. They school together in large shoals of hundreds or thousands of individuals. Although generally thought to be solitary hunters on the prowl for food, some studies suggest that, in some cases, barracuda may act co-operatively to scatter schools of fish so as to pick off the scattered individuals.

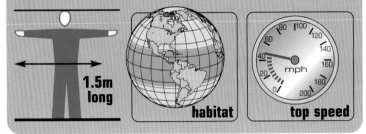

1.5m long

habitat

top speed

me a chance to see them right up close, however. Their eyes are very large for their size, as sight is one of their more important senses. I couldn't help looking at those huge sharp teeth though, especially when the fish chomped the bait in half before swallowing it. Compared to the normal fishy shape, the barracuda is a real racing dragster. It has got a very thin aerodynamic body and a large, powerful tail. It is the classic little car with a big engine. And it's got racing stripes.

In between feeding bouts the fish would move closer to the surface and at one point I saw them have a bit of a territorial scrap. They looked like silver arrows lancing through the water towards each other. Their acceleration was the most amazing thing. They can accelerate to a top speed of 45 miles per hour in under a second, which knocks a Ferrari's acceleration into a cocked hat.

After being fed a few fish the barracuda calmed right down, so Brian let me feed them by hand. I was a little nervous to start with, but they were very gentle and took the fish expertly from my fingers without ever coming near to biting me by mistake.

After we had finished filming and were back on shore we received a radio call from Captain Slate's boat. Brian had been feeding the barracuda again and had been bitten quite badly. We rushed out to collect him in a speedboat and brought him to shore. His hand was already bandaged up, but he said it was a mess and that he would need quite a number of stitches. He actually seemed quite pleased. Being scarred in his line of work is like receiving a medal.

He had been feeding two barracuda and was watching one, but the other sped in and tried to take the bait first. He never saw a thing, his hand was just surrounded by a cloud of blood. He hardly even felt it until he got out of the water.

I felt very relieved that I was leaving this place with all my fingers intact. The barracuda isn't a fish to mess with.

Below: One barracuda had bitten through the whole side of Captain Slate's mask.

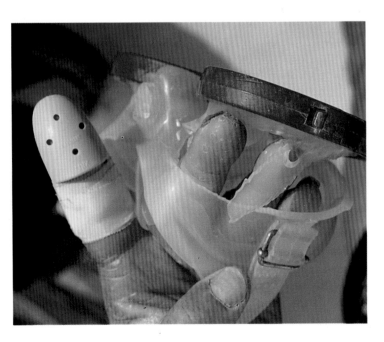

blue marlin

If you are going to be the fastest on the block you are going to need room to manoeuvre. For the fastest fish in the sea there is no bigger space to burn rubber than the open oceans. We chose the US Virgin Islands as the base from which we would sail out into the wide Atlantic Ocean in search of the legendary marlin. There are many species of marlin and they are all fast, but we were most likely to find blue marlin in these waters. They may not be the quickest fish in the world, but they are still spectacularly fast.

Now I'm not a big fan of fishing and rarely have I held a fishing rod. Even more rarely have I ever caught a fish, let alone one that could be the weight of a small horse. However, sport fishing is big business in these waters and whether you agree with it or not, it is the main lobby for conservation in the face of ever-decreasing fish numbers.

Large billfish such as the marlin are getting rarer and rarer and there could be many factors that have contributed towards their decline. Pollution and commercial fishing are the most likely causes, however, and the sports fishermen and fisherwomen are getting worried.

The main problem is that little is known about the nature of these animals. How long do they live? Do they migrate? These questions need to be answered in order to manage successfully those fish still left.

Where once a large trophy fish was hauled back to shore and displayed for all to see on the harbour, sports fishing now has a more sustainable feel to it. More often than not marlin are tagged and released. Important data is starting to appear from subsequent catches of tagged fish. One fish was caught near New Zealand, 7,000 miles away from its original tagging point. Tagging was started in the Virgin Islands by a number of concerned people, including Captain Red, the man who was acting as our guide.

To tag a fish you have to catch it and it was down to me to do the catching. We powered out in Captain Red's boat, the *Abigail III*, to the deep waters of the Atlantic where the marlin like to hunt. In fact, the deepest waters in these parts are over five miles deep.

Opposite: Marlin hunt in the deep waters of the Atlantic.

Right: Brightly coloured lures are meant to resemble real squid.

me feeling a little nervous, but Red and Donovan reassured me I would be fine.

To increase our chances of success we cast out four lines. On the end of each was a lure in the shape of a squid. If there are real squid as colourful as these were, they have yet to be discovered. With the lines dragging behind us we settled in for a long wait. The swell in the open ocean was a little too much for some of our film crew, so they spent a few hours lying down and turning subtle shades of green.

It seemed as if we had trawled for hours when suddenly one of the reels started screaming. Donovan was on the rod in a flash and I was in the chair. He struck the rod a few times to make sure the fish was hooked before handing it to me. It was all I could do to hang on to it. The line it had pulled out in those few seconds was phenomenal. It had obviously run a long way and I had to reel it back in. Donovan and Red had to wind in the other lures before we went any further, as we could only manage one fish at a time, although they have had three on the go at once before.

My arms were straining hard to keep the rod upright until Donovan clipped the harness I was sitting in onto the reel. I could then use my body weight to pull the rod up and start to reel in. The technique is to pull up slowly and then wind the reel as you drop the rod quickly. It takes a lot of leg power and co-ordination. I had just started to reel in when the fish burst out of the water behind us and arced through the air. It looked incredible with the huge, sharp bill at the front and that massively powerful crescent-shaped tail at the back.

Then the line went slack. My fish spat the lure out and escaped. Donovan had estimated it at 250 pounds from its size. We reset the lures and settled down again. I was disappointed, but Donovan said I had done well and that it was just one of those things.

We had another long wait before the

The *Abigail III* is a very plush boat and superbly equipped. Massive rods and reels adorn the back half of the boat and in the centre is the throne. The latter is a huge swivelling chair from which the fish is reeled in when hooked. Captain Red talked me through the correct technique and introduced me to Donovan, who was to be my wireman. His job was to grab the line when the fish gets close and manoeuvre it alongside the boat.

Now, to ensure the fish is to survive it is imperative that it doesn't get too tired, so it has to be brought in quickly. This had

Above: Reeling in 350 pounds of fish was hard enough, but blue marlin can weigh nearly six times this weight.

next bite, so we were all a little unprepared for it when it happened. I leapt into the chair as Donovan wrestled with the rod, but this fish spat the lure before he could hand me the rod. There was still a chance that it might bite again or that there was another fish with it that would, so Donovan held onto his rod. Suddenly the rod next to me bent double and the reel started screaming. Donovan still had his hands full so I lifted it out of its holder to strike the fish. I was nearly dragged off the back of the boat by the power of the thing. The pull of this fish was even stronger and it had taken even more of the line out. I jumped back in the chair, clipped myself in and started working to bring it in. Tales of three-hour battles ran through my head and I hoped I had the stamina to last out.

What followed was like a twenty-minute thrash on a rowing machine. Uphill. I was having to really work hard to reel in the hundreds of feet of line that the fish had

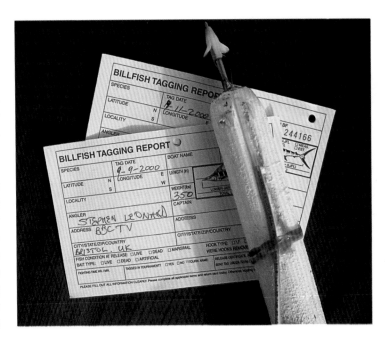

Above: Tagging may provide vital information to help ensure the marlin's survival.

spooled out. It had dived deep down and was not keen on coming up. Just as I could see the start of the lure line, the fish dived and dragged a load more line out again. Red and Donovan were willing me on, coaching me and encouraging me to keep going, but I was drowning in sweat and my thigh muscles were burning with each exhausting stroke.

Finally I saw the lure line reach the end of the rod and Donovan grabbed it with gloved hands and raised the thrashing marlin alongside the boat. It was a nice specimen, weighing an estimated 350 pounds. Red was already there with the tagging pole and the fish was quickly tagged. I leapt out of the chair and managed to get a look at it before it freed itself from my hook and disappeared.

Who knows where it will speed off to and if, or where, it will be caught again? Hopefully, something will come from this programme that will enable these fish to remain in these waters, because the world would be a much duller place without them.

BLUE MARLIN (makaira nigricans)

The blue marlin belongs to a group of fish that includes tuna, swordfish, spearfish and sailfish. Marlin are solitary hunters of the open ocean and make annual migrations of thousands of miles. They have a wide distribution but are thought to be generally scarce. Marlin are believed to be the fastest fish in the oceans, reaching speeds of 45mph (72km/h) for blue marlin and 81mph (130km/h) for the black marlin (*Makaira indica*). A number of factors help marlin to achieve speed. A streamlined body shape with fins that fold into grooves flat against the body to reduce drag; fewer yet tougher caudal vertebrae than in other fish allow greater thrust to be transferred from the tail to the body. The tail itself is long and thin, providing greater thrust with less drag. Pacific and Atlantic marlin feed largely on skipjack tuna. They can use their bills to slash through schools of tuna, picking off the injured ones. Marlin can weigh 2,000lb (909kg) and grow to 13ft (4m) in length. They are thought to live for about twenty years.

4m long

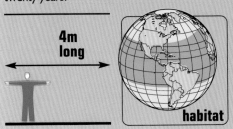

habitat   top speed

northern gannet

These speedy seabirds can be found along many coastlines, but one of their most spectacular haunts is found just off the coast of North Berwick, Scotland.

Bass Rock is a huge pinnacle of rock jutting straight out of the sea about a mile from the mainland. It was originally formed from a volcanic core and evidence of the fault it lies upon is still visible. On its cliffs

Bass Rock has the ruins of a fourteenth-century fortress that was converted into a prison. More recently built was the lighthouse, which up until 1988 was manned. The island is still inhabited, though – by gannets, currently 40,000 of them.

Fred Marr, a local boatman, took us out to the island in his wooden launch. He has been running trips and fishing these waters for over fifty years. From the harbour the rock looks as white as chalk, but as you get closer you can make out that it is virtually all birds. Fred remembers when there were five acres of grass on the top of the island, but the birds have increased in number to such an extent that the grass has long been covered. I have seen gannets before, but never as many as this. The sky seemed to be full of them, but that was nothing compared with the number on the rock.

The next thing you notice after the number is the smell. Ammonia fills the air downwind of the island, because of all the droppings. As we climbed onto the island I saw that everything was painted with the droppings and I knew that by the end of the day I would be too.

We had a huge amount of kit to carry up the paths to where the birds were nesting. We ferried it to the start of the nesting area up a long narrow path and onto the top of the island.

Every scrap of rock had a nest on it. Space is something these birds don't have, and so is tolerance. If a bird strays more than a few inches from its spot it is pecked mercilessly by its neighbours. Gannets' beaks are mean-looking weapons and they

didn't seem too worried about using them on my legs as I passed. Thankfully I was usually out of reach and so evaded injury.

The nests were inhabited by young gannets of all ages. Some birds still had eggs while the offspring of others had almost fledged. Fully grown, the chicks are slightly bigger than their parents, leaving even less room to spare.

The weather forecast had predicted showers, but apart from a slight drizzle on the way over we were doing okay. However, as soon as the camera was turned on the heavens opened and the rain didn't let up until we left.

The birds seemed to be very graceful in the air, but as soon as they came to land they flew with all the finesse of house bricks. They came in to land far too quickly and simply splatted down on the rock. They often landed on their neighbours, who gave them a fairly brutal welcome.

All that changed later in the afternoon, though, because the wind picked up. The gannets came in riding the wind, able to hover stationary inches above the rock. Floating there in front of me, I could

Above: High winds allow the gannets to hover over their nests for gentler landings.

Below and opposite: Bass Rock is popular with the gannets and not a scrap of space is wasted.

clearly see the adaptations they have for fast flying. The wings are long and thin with stiff feathers. It seems that they are so refined for speed that they need the high winds to achieve safe take-offs and landings. Indeed, to launch themselves for the first time, the chicks have to get to the cliff's edge and throw themselves off. The fall enables them to build up enough speed to allow them to gain control. However, a high percentage of birds get it completely wrong and the rocks are littered with their carcasses.

But the gannets' ungainliness on the land is more than made up for by their skill and speed when hunting over the open water. This is one bird that likes its sushi kamikaze-style.

Our mission was to try and encourage the gannets to perform their death-defying dives for us. Payment for this was mackerel, which is the natural diet of these birds. Mackerel are fast, powerful predators in their own right and, in fact, the gannet is the only aerial predator fast enough to catch them.

As soon as we got close to the rock,

NORTHERN GANNET (morus bassanus)

Gannets have a wingspan of 5.2–5.9ft (1.6–1.8m). They are designed for diving and feed on fish such as herring and mackerel. They have good binocular vision, which they use to spot their prey as they circle overhead. Once they have locked onto the prey, they plummet from heights of up to 98ft (30m) and hit the water at speeds of up to 90mph (145km/h). They fold back their wings (to prevent damage) just over 0.8 seconds before they hit the water, and dive into the water like a torpedo. Various features enable gannets to withstand the impact of hitting the water at such speeds: a toughened skull, leathery eyelids and inflatable air sacs in the neck and upper chest all serve to cushion the bird, and internal nostrils prevent water flooding into the lungs. These birds often dive to 13ft (4m), swallowing small fish whole and bringing larger ones to the surface. Britain has around 201,000 pairs of breeding northern gannets (70% of the world's population). Outside Britain they breed in the North Atlantic in an arc from eastern maritime Canada to Norway.

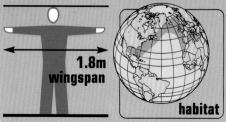

1.8m wingspan

habitat

top speed

Fred's son, Chris, started cutting up mackerel and tossing it overboard. Initially it was the gulls that swooped in to claim the free meal. However, as the fish pieces sank, it was pretty soon out of their reach. It would have to sink a fair way before it was out of reach of the gannets, however. Unlike the gulls that splashed down onto the surface, just dipping their heads underwater, the gannets hit the water at full speed, wings tucked behind them. Their momentum allowed them to zip right through the water down to the deeper fish. They can dive to depths of 30 feet to claim their fishy prize. The visibility through the water was excellent and I could see them lancing through the water like torpedoes.

All their lack of grace on the rock was forgiven. The gannets' accuracy and timing are unparalleled. Their whole design is geared to this unique talent. Excellent vision allows them to spot fish deep under

Opposite: Gannets have toughened skulls which enable them to dive at speed. **Below:** With their extreme design and phenomenal timing, gannets are able to hit the water at incredibly high speeds – a feat that would kill most other birds.

the water. They stall their speed, using their wings to hover above the fish at a height of up to 100 feet. They then roll and dive straight down, accelerating to a speed of 60 miles per hour or more before they hit the water. While descending they can still steer until the last moment, when they rake their wings back to avoid damage. The timing of this manoeuvre is critical, because if they leave it too late they could fatally injure themselves. Pure instinct drives the whole sequence and ensures the bird's body responds at just the right time, like a computer-driven machine.

Gannets are so aerodynamic that they hardly make a splash, but the impact still has to be fairly substantial. Their skulls are built like crash helmets and they inflate air sacs round the throat to cushion the blow.

To see all this evolutionary refinement in action was fantastic. The whole movement was completely fluid and effortless. When we threw the remaining pieces of fish overboard we were treated to formation diving of up to six birds at a time, which was spectacular to behold.

Returning to the mainland, we left the island glowing white in the sun and the sound of 40,000 gannets followed us nearly all the way home.

peregrine falcon
ULTIMATE KILLER

It seemed strange that we had to fly to Spain to see a peregrine falcon in flight. Especially as Lady, the peregrine in question, normally lives just outside Bristol. Lloyd Buck, her handler, has had her for five years and has trained her to pursue a yellow beanbag as a lure. It was Lloyd's idea to strap this lure to a skydiver's arm and see if she could catch it. Skydivers fall at about 120 miles per hour. Could the peregrine keep up with us at this sort of speed? To enable us to skydive with the peregrine we had to jump from a balloon, so we needed good, predictable weather. And that was the reason we went to Spain.

The plan was fairly simple. We would climb to 10,000 feet and I would tandem skydive with Andy Montriou, a very experienced skydiver. He would be carrying the yellow beanbag lure in his hand for Lady to chase. Leo Dickinson, our cameraman, was going to accompany us on the skydive, with three cameras strapped to his head to catch the action. There were also numerous cameras strapped to the balloon to get footage of us as we all left the safety of the basket.

The complicated part was recovering everything on the ground. We parachutists would land in one place, the balloonists in another and Lady in a third. We had three vehicles on the ground in radio contact. The hardest to locate would be Lady, but Lloyd had fitted her with a radio transmitter and Lee Sparey, another experienced raptor handler, was on the ground with a receiver.

Everybody climbed inside the basket except for Andy and me. We were in economy class, which consisted of a wooden

platform on the outside. We were attached to the basket by straps, but it was a very exposed position.

As the balloon left the ground, I became a little nervous. I don't suffer from vertigo much, but I wasn't comfortable. Funnily though, the higher we went the less fear I had. It was probably because I knew we could parachute down. The views were spectacular and in between the roaring of the burners it was really still and quiet. It had been cold on the ground but up there, higher than the snow-capped mountains, it was below freezing.

Above: Andy and I stood on a wooden platform as the balloon rose to 10,000 feet.

Opposite: It still is not fully understood how such a light bird can reach the speeds it does.

We really struggled to reach our jump height and were drifting towards the mountains – basically, we were too heavy and it was taking us too long to climb. When we got to 10,000 feet, Leo leapt up onto the edge of the balloon. Andy was scanning the ground uneasily and, to be honest, I was crapping myself. At the last moment Andy said 'No jump'. It was too unsafe. The ground was uneven and forested, so landing would be too dangerous. Dave Seager-Thomas, our balloon pilot, took us gently down. Landing in a balloon can be a hair-raising experience, but we touched down very gracefully.

Weight became a very big issue now. We all tripped down to the local chemists to weigh ourselves. Martin Hughes-Games, the series producer, was the only person who had lied about his weight and was thoroughly chastized for it. We stripped the basket of all non-essential equipment and passengers and launched at the next available window of good weather.

At 10,000 feet Andy, Leo and Dave, the balloon pilot, were scanning below us to see if it was safe to jump. Any moment now, I thought, and it would be all called off. So I was a little surprised when, after a lengthy discussion, Andy said, 'Let's do it.' I could not believe it. The moment of truth. To be completely honest, I was petrified, but I knew I had to go. I unclipped my harness from the basket and slowly Andy and I turned round. I now had nothing between me and the ground, except 10,000 feet of open space. My toes were hanging off the platform and I could only hang onto a strap behind me with one hand. Andy's next comment was 'Pick your feet up, Steve.' This was it – my life in his hands. I arched back, just as we had practised on the ground, and reluctantly released my grip on the strap behind me.

Lloyd had unhooded Lady and Leo was standing on the basket edge. Andy, Leo, Lady and I were all perched, waiting on Lloyd's command. The yellow lure was in Andy's hand and Lady was blinking in the light, searching for it. Only when she had a good fix on it would we go.

'Wait! Wait! Wait!' Lloyd shouted. It seemed like an eternity as I stared up into the blue sky above before he bellowed, 'Camera! Ready! Steady! . . . Go!'

We tipped forward and hurtled head-first, straight down. Andy had told me that jumping from a balloon is very different to jumping from a plane. You really get a sensation of falling, because you start from stationary in a balloon. We levelled out into a freefall position and I immediately started looking for Lady. Leo was bearing in on us, but there was no Lady. The lure was still in Andy's hand right until just before deployment when he had had to let it go.

After feeling a huge braking sensation pulling on my harness, Andy announced

PEREGRINE FALCON (falco peregrinus)

The fastest flying bird in the world is the peregrine falcon. It is built for speed: short wings with narrow tips reduce drag; when held back, the wings minimize turbulence and resistance so they can slice through the air; the tail acts as a rudder for steering when spread and provides excellent control. As they stoop or plunge-dive from a height to catch prey, peregrines reach speeds of 200mph (320km/h). During level flight they average 31mph (50km/h). Peregrines feed almost exclusively on birds such as ducks and herons that they take in the air. Diving from great heights they strike the prey with their talons or bite the victim's neck to ensure death. Juvenile peregrines begin hunting when they are nine to twelve weeks old, taking dragonflies and butterflies. The peregrine falcon has a wide distribution and is found on all continents, except Antarctica. Usually found in areas of open space, nesting on high cliffs and bluffs, it has also adapted to artificial environments and can be found in cities with tall buildings. Peregrines grow to 15–20in (38–50cm) in length, with wingspans of around 18in (45cm) for average females. Females are generally about one-third bigger than males with an average weight of approximately 2lb (1kg).

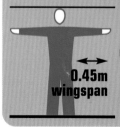

0.45m
wingspan

habitat

top speed

Right: It took half an hour to rise to 10,000 feet in the balloon. Andy and I took only 42 seconds to freefall to 3,000 feet, where we opened the parachute.

that we were under a perfectly good canopy. Leo had deployed much lower and was circling towards the agreed landing zone. As we spun round I checked the skies for Lady, with no success. Leo made a perfect landing and radioed up to us to let us know the lie of the land.

But what of Lady's performance? It was her first attempt at chasing tandem sky-divers and she had hesitated slightly. However, she had caught the lure before it hit the ground. Considering that it had

been travelling in Andy's hand at an average speed of 138 miles per hour with a maximum of 145 miles per hour, according to our speedometer, that wasn't bad. In fact, the whole thing had worked fantastically despite Lady not getting the lure out of Andy's hand. The recovery of the falcon, the balloon and ourselves had gone like clockwork.

Lady wasn't keen on chasing Andy and me together, as we had to have a small parachute open during freefall to slow us down.

It was decided to give her another chance just chasing Andy on his own.

I had to watch from the ground as Andy, Leo and Lady left the balloon. Through binoculars I could see them accelerate downwards at a phenomenal rate. They deployed their parachutes and I set off in the car to pick them up. I came upon Leo and Andy by the road quite quickly. They were both stunned by their experience. Andy had left first, backwards, swiftly followed by Lady and then Leo. Lady had stayed within 10 feet of Andy for the first half of the jump, swooping in to grab the lure from his hand. Even though he was hurtling down at over 150 miles per hour, Andy said that Lady had come towards him as if he were stationary. He added that he had never experienced anything like it before while skydiving,

and he has done over 4,500 jumps.

Lee was having problems finding Lady, who caught the lure after Andy released it. Eventually he found her settled in a small copse of trees across a field. She was very pleased with herself and was chirping away, having ripped open the bean bag.

We viewed the footage back in the hotel on a big television. Lady had leapt off Lloyd's fist and pumped her wings as she flew straight down at Andy. After about two or three flaps she went into what is called a 'mummy wrap', in which she folded her wings right round her. From Leo's head camera you could see her in this position, quickly gaining on him – and he was doing over 120 miles per hour. It was one of the most incredible things I have ever seen. She truly deserves the title of an Ultimate Speed Killer.

Opposite: Split-second timing for the free-fall dive was absolutely crucial.
Below: Lady was fairly unimpressed by our 145mph race.

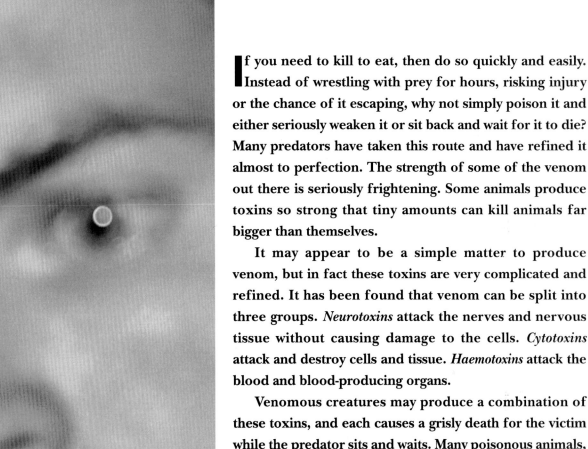

venom

If you need to kill to eat, then do so quickly and easily. Instead of wrestling with prey for hours, risking injury or the chance of it escaping, why not simply poison it and either seriously weaken it or sit back and wait for it to die? Many predators have taken this route and have refined it almost to perfection. The strength of some of the venom out there is seriously frightening. Some animals produce toxins so strong that tiny amounts can kill animals far bigger than themselves.

It may appear to be a simple matter to produce venom, but in fact these toxins are very complicated and refined. It has been found that venom can be split into three groups. *Neurotoxins* attack the nerves and nervous tissue without causing damage to the cells. *Cytotoxins* attack and destroy cells and tissue. *Haemotoxins* attack the blood and blood-producing organs.

Venomous creatures may produce a combination of these toxins, and each causes a grisly death for the victim while the predator sits and waits. Many poisonous animals, whether by accident or in defence, can use their venom on humans and it is these that we have concentrated on in this chapter. Although we may not be their prey, these animals kill thousands of people a year all over the world. Some may escape death but are left with horrific legacies of their encounters. I spoke to a number of people who had suffered greatly from poisonous bites or stings and even experienced some myself. These animals are not to be taken lightly and although a lot of them are small, they all pack a serious punch.

komodo dragon

The komodo dragon is probably the most geographically isolated large carnivore on the planet. Living on a handful of islands within Indonesia, it escaped western attention until 1912, except for a few maps with the legend 'Here be Dragons'.

I had seen photos and film footage of these dragons, but now I was about to meet them face to face. Well, hopefully not that close, given how bad their breath is meant to be. As a spectacle for tourists, the dragons used to be fed, but the practice stopped in 1996 as they had become reliant on free meals and had stopped hunting for themselves.

On the day that we filmed, one very dead wild boar was on the menu, an animal that thrives on Komodo Island. It was early morning and there were no dragons in sight. The rich smell would attract them from miles around, but first the dragons would have to warm up in the morning sun before they became active. We set up the filming gear and waited.

It wasn't long before our first big lizard joined us. I had expected komodos to move slowly and drag their bellies, but when properly warmed up they are a lot friskier than that. This one was a biggish female and was running swiftly towards us, carrying her body quite high.

My first impression was 'Look at the size of that thing!' I knew komodo dragons were big, but it's only when you see them

Opposite: Virulent bacteria in their saliva gives the komodo dragon's bite a very nasty effect.

Right: With its massive tongue, the dragon sniffs out a potential meal.

in real life that you get a true perspective of their massive size. Head to tail this one was about 6 feet and very solidly built. It had a brutish-looking face, a blunt nose and the most amazing tongue I have ever seen. When it flicked its tongue out at full length it was as long as its head and highly manoeuvrable.

Komodo dragons are very primitive animals and are not fussy about what they eat. This female knew there was food to be had

Above: Incredibly sharp teeth make short work of the thick boar hide.

in the area because of the smell, but she wasn't sure exactly where, so she ran straight for us.

Despite the appalling smell, the boar had only been dead a day or so and the female dragon had a real job trying to tear the tough skin to get at the meat inside. Try as she might she couldn't find a way. What she needed was a helping hand.

Assistance was soon supplied in the shape of a massive male. I thought the female was big until I saw this guy. He was absolutely huge, with a thick, strong neck and powerful forelimbs armed with wicked-looking claws.

After a reasonable attempt at eating us, he ambled over to the boar, opened his mouth and engulfed the animal's head in one go. He wasn't able to do much more than the female, but now he had a really good grip she was able to climb over him and somehow rip the boar's belly open. Another male arrived on the scene and things got very messy, as both he and the female climbed over the giant male to eviscerate the boar.

The biggest dragon proceeded to try and swallow the whole boar in one. It was just too big, despite the fact that he was able to disarticulate his jaw like a snake. The other two continued to rip out all the boar's innards and feast on its back legs. The noise was amazing. Crunching, tearing, hissing and gulping. There was also a harsh rasping sound from the komodos' scaly hides rubbing together as they clambered over each other. They showed no regard for each other at all as they stood on each other's heads and occasionally bit each other in their attempts to get at the juiciest morsels.

It took ages for them to reduce the carcass to the last few mouthfuls. In that time another largish male joined the party. The giant had still got the head end, but had worked it down his massive throat to near the rib cage. The others had all but eaten

Below: A very powerful and intimidating creature.

KOMODO DRAGON (varanus komodoensis)

The komodo dragon is the world's largest lizard – males can grow up to 6.6ft (2m) long and can live for about 50 years. Weight varies depending on when it last fed, but the hunting weight of an average komodo dragon is about 550lb (250kg). They live on the Indonesian islands of Komodo, Rinca, Gili Motang and Nusa Kode. Komodo dragons have a mouth full of bacteria – so far sixty-two different types have been identified. These bacteria cause septicaemia and are so powerful that one type can kill an animal such as a goat or buffalo in eight hours; many of the other types can cause death within seventy-two hours. Komodo dragons use their bacteria in much the same way venomous snakes use their venom. If they are unable to kill the prey animal outright, the infection caused by the bacteria will often be enough to either kill the animal or weaken it sufficiently that it become easy pickings within a couple of days. Komodo dragons are capable of eating up to 80% of their starved body weight in one sitting. They typically feed on deer, wild pigs and water buffalo, although adults will also cannibalize young komodo dragons. There have been six fatal attacks on humans.

2m long

habitat

08:00:00
HR MIN SEC

time to death after bite

the back half. Eventually, when he thought he could manage it, the male lifted his head and gulped the remainder down, with the other dragons trying to grab what they could before it all disappeared.

During their meal they were totally focused on eating and we could almost stand between them. Once or twice I had to be careful not to stand on a tail.

For some reason I thought that after such a big feast the dragons would slope off into the shade to digest it. Again my preconceptions proved to be incorrect. The komodos were still hungry and considered us fair game. It is quite intimidating to have the largest lizards in the world coming at you with dinner on their minds. Thankfully the rangers fended them off with their poles while we made our escape.

The threat to us was a real one and indeed there are a number of accounts of people being killed and eaten by the dragons. We met a small boy called Harry at the village on Komodo Island who'd had a very lucky escape. Harry was attacked by a dragon when he was only nine years old. He was walking along a path when the dragon leapt out and grabbed him by his arm. He fought to get away and the dragon bit him on his other arm. Luckily his friends heard his cries and came to his aid. After scaring the dragon away by throwing stones, they managed to get him home. He was brought to a doctor on another island who stitched his wounds and, more importantly, gave him antibiotics. He was feverish for one week and it took him a full month to recover completely. Without treatment, he would probably have died, because although the dragons don't have a proper venom they still have a deadly bite.

Bacteria cultivated in the komodos' mouths are used as a very primitive venom.

Some of the species of bacteria are the same as you would find in my, or anybody else's, throat, but they are extremely virulent strains. When the komodos ambush their prey they often bite it a couple of times and then let it escape, especially with big prey such as buffalo. However, the bite wounds eventually become infected with the dragon's lethal bacteria and fester. The infection becomes so bad that it can kill the animal in a few days. Smaller prey can take as little as seven hours to die from septicaemia (blood-poisoning). All the komodo dragon has to do is follow the injured animal and wait for the bacteria to do its work.

Thankfully the bacteria haven't had exposure to antibiotics and are easily dealt with. That is why Harry is alive today.

brown recluse spider

Spiders are found pretty much everywhere, but we needed a real heavyweight. Consequently I found myself sharing a motel room in Texas, USA, with the biggest species of spider on the planet.

It was a *Theraphosa blondi*, known locally as the 'gigantic bird eater', even though it doesn't eat birds. This example was female; they grow much larger than the males. Martin, the series producer, is a real spider lover and has a pet tarantula at home. He was very reassuring about handling the spider and informed me that its bite wasn't dangerous. He admitted that nobody had been recorded as being bitten by one, so I remained uncertain as to how he knew that it wasn't dangerous.

The spider was placed on a pillow on the bed and I was to turn and pick it up. I was shocked to hear quite a loud hissing noise from the spider when I handled it. It makes this noise by rubbing hairs together. These are not the only special hairs that it possesses, either. Gigantic bird eaters have irritant hairs called 'urticating setae', which they brush off with their legs into the air towards potential attackers. These hairs are barbed and can cause a fair degree of discomfort in sensitive areas such as eyes, nose and mouth. I ended up with them embedded in my palm, which was slightly itchy for the remainder of the day.

My first few attempts at picking the *blondi* up were a bit tentative. I was worried about how it would react and also didn't want to end up hurting it. However, with each successive time my confidence grew and I think it started to trust me a little. Before me, it had hardly been handled at all (another cheerful piece of information from Martin). Anyway, we were getting on fine.

The weight of this spider proved to me just how solid it was. It was such a strange sensation as it crept over my hands. I could feel tiny pincers at the end of each of its legs gripping my skin.

Getting it onto my hands was the easy part. All I had to do was to scoop my hands underneath it and let it walk on. Getting a look at its fangs was not as simple. I had to balance it on one hand, which wasn't easy, as it was bigger than my palm. Then I had to grab it with the other hand and turn it upside down. It was a good handful to hold but it didn't struggle at all. It just tucked up its legs and stayed perfectly still. When not attacking prey or defending itself, the *blondi*'s fangs are folded neatly either side of its mouth. From underneath I could see them quite clearly and they were pretty impressive. I didn't want to be the first person to receive a good stab from them, that was for sure.

Nevertheless, even given the size of the *blondi's* fangs, I would rather have a bite from her than a bite from the spider I was subsequently given inside a matchbox. In fact I wasn't even allowed to handle this spider. It was a brown recluse spider and despite its innocuous looks, it is a creature to treat with a healthy level of respect. This small brown, average-looking spider has a very nasty bite. It releases a cocktail of unpleasant chemicals in its venom that

Opposite: The *Theraphosa blondi* is the largest spider on the planet.

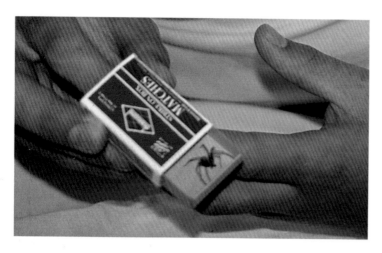

destroys skin, fat and blood cells. Even a tiny amount can lead to massive tissue loss (one woman had to have a basketball's diameter of flesh removed after a bite), amputation of a limb or, in extreme cases, death from gangrene or kidney failure.

The brown recluse spider is found quite commonly in the southeast of the USA in

Above: The brown recluse spider can be found in all sorts of nooks and crannies, resulting in a high incidence of bites.

BROWN RECLUSE SPIDER (loxosceles reclusa)

Recluse spiders belong to a family of six-eyed spiders (rather than the usual eight) found in North America, Central and South America and South Africa. There are thirteen species of recluse spiders in North America, five of which have been implicated in human poisonings. The most noted is the brown recluse, which is 0.4–0.5in (10–12mm) long. Adults live for up to two years. Markings on its back have given rise to the common names 'fiddleback' or 'violin' spider. Brown recluse spiders live in webs of sticky silk and often inhabit attics, barns and cellars, so their lifestyle brings them into close contact with people. There appear to be several components to the venom. One causes local skin necrosis (death of cells), while another destroys red blood cells. Another causes clotting, while another destroys fat cells below the skin. The end result is a black, gangrenous spot. Often the skin starts to peel away, exposing underlying tissues; in extreme cases this can result in a 6in (15cm) wound. Between 1960 and 1969 six human deaths were attributed to the brown recluse spider in the USA, while in 1990, in South Carolina alone, there were 478 reported bites.

12mm long

habitat

00:00:00
HR MIN SEC

many attacks, death rare

wood or rock piles, but can also be found in houses, garages and sheds. Bites are relatively common but most result in one-off ulcers and minor scarring.

After a short ride on a hired Harley Davidson I ended up in Luckenbach, a dusty wooden-shacked town in the middle of nowhere. I was there to meet two people whose lives had taken a real bad turn when they met the brown recluse.

A rare complication of the recluse bite is recurrent ulceration at the bite site or elsewhere on the body. Robin McCutchan was bitten on the hand in June 1999 while sweeping up at work. She has had about thirty or forty lesions break out since then on her hands and legs. She has excruciating pain with each new lesion and is left with a new scar every time. The longest she has been without a lesion is only two to three weeks. When she has the lesions her hands are too painful to do anything, even change her son's nappies. Her father had the same response to a bite on his hand fourteen years ago. He had recurrent lesions for two years. Robin is worried that this response to the spider bite may be hereditary and that her son is at risk too.

LeeAnn Parkes was bitten ten years ago and is still suffering. Two years after the bite she had half her finger amputated because she was told it was the only way to finally get rid of the problem. Eight years and twenty-one doctors later she is still suffering repeated bouts of horrific ulceration. Each time the stump of her finger ulcerates it exposes bone and the pain is unbelievable. Most of the doctors she has seen have had no success at all in helping her with her condition. She showed me photos of the last time she had an outbreak. I could clearly see the bone sticking out of the end of her finger. I am used to seeing horrific wounds, but I couldn't help recoiling at the thought of the pain involved. One of the last doctors to examine her

Left: LeeAnn had never seen another brown recluse spider since she was bitten by one ten years ago.

LeeAnn introduced Robin to the stun gun treatment and it seems to have helped her as well. They met over the Internet on a page set up to help recluse spider bite victims. The two women are very emotional about the fact that they found each other as they had previously suffered in isolation. Alone they had no voice, but with further sufferers getting in touch they hope to lobby for greater research into their condition.

I had a couple of the brown recluse spiders in clear plastic pots with me and LeeAnn asked to have a closer look at one. Her hands were visibly trembling as she looked at the first brown recluse spider she had seen since the one that bit her ten years ago. I was amazed at her bravery. It is astonishing to think that such a small spider had caused her a decade of pain and suffering.

suggested the amputation of her hand at the wrist. LeeAnn is an ICU nurse and could not practise without her hand.

The only thing that has helped LeeAnn is a controversial treatment advocated by one Dr Abrams, a retired practitioner in the States. He modified a police stun gun to deliver a slightly lower voltage and used the electric shock across the last ulcer. LeeAnn was submitted to fifteen shocks, some up her arm and some directly across the exposed tissue of the wound. The ulcer, which would usually have taken six weeks to heal, was healed in eight days. LeeAnn gave me three blasts of the stun gun on my arm. It was an extremely painful and unpleasant experience. I cannot imagine what it must be like when applied to exposed tissue, but LeeAnn told me that it was nothing when compared to the pain associated with the full ulcer.

Right: The brown recluse spider may look innocuous but it has a very nasty cocktail of toxins in its venom.

scorpion

To film scorpions we could have gone to a lot of places in the world. But we needed an enthusiastic expert and we could do no better than Major Scott Stockwell in San Antonio, Texas.

Scott is a medical entomologist for the US Army, so his job usually entails teaching soldiers how to prevent diseases spread by biting insects such as mosquitoes, the infamous spreaders of malaria. Occasionally he gets to talk about his favourite subject – scorpions.

We met Scott in his teaching room at Fort Sam Houston base in San Antonio, where he was giving a lecture to some of his students. The room is full of large models of insects and, more impressively, aquariums housing massive spiders. Scott is a great teacher and really keeps his audience riveted, bringing out all manner of specimens to shock the class. He even keeps a couple of scorpions in his pocket to drop into students' hands.

The scorpion cases are held in an incubator to keep them more comfortable. It didn't take Scott too long to dig a few out for us to look at. First he produced an animal that is commonly confused with a scorpion, called a vinegarroon. It doesn't have a sting at all but has claws and a long thin tail-like appendage, so you could be forgiven for mixing the two up. People often kill it needlessly, which is a shame as it is completely harmless.

The emperor scorpion from West Africa wins hands down in the competition for most impressive-looking scorpion. It is very large and blackish in colour. Scott placed a female on my hand for me to get a close look. I am not really afraid of spiders or insects, but this did send a bit of shiver down my back. Each foot has a tiny pair of pincers to hold on with and I could feel them lightly gripping me. I had fully expected an immediate attack from it as soon as it hit my hand, but they are remarkably relaxed creatures. I was surprised at the weight of it, even given its size.

The emperor scorpion isn't deadly at all, as it relies on its tremendous claws, which are powerful enough to draw blood from a human, to kill its prey. They do have stings and one used its sting on Scott, who said it was comparable to a bee sting. He didn't react much to it, but he has been stung many times before by far worse scorpions.

The next scorpion was from closer to Texas. Scott had collected a box full of Arizonian hairy scorpions. These were much smaller and less impressive than the emperors, but pack a much worse punch. The toxicity of their venom is greater and stings are common. These were the first scorpions I picked up by myself. The technique is to grab them either side of the sting between finger and thumb and lift them up. If done correctly this stops them from being able to sting you, but they can still grab you with their claws, which is also pretty painful.

That is the best method, but it didn't stop Scott simply scooping up the whole lot in his hands. He didn't get stung at all, which showed they need a lot of harassment before they will sting. In case this wasn't clear enough he tipped them all into my hand. Some of them landed with a thud

Opposite: Scorpions are fairly laid-back and need a lot of provocation to sting.

flew right above him and it was then that I realized how big she was. She utterly dwarfed him hanging there just below the nest. She then flew off to another tree to watch us from a distance.

I started climbing up the ropes. I began quickly, but soon realized it was a lot further than I thought, and so settled into a steadier rhythm. I was really sweating when I reached the nest. I peeped over the edge and came face to face with the chick. It was about the size of a chicken, with fluffy white feathers. It had its mum's beak and feet though, which looked almost comical on such a small bird.

I had been happy trusting the climbing ropes, but I now had to trust harpy architecture. The nest was about 2 metres wide and the same in depth. I had to shimmy round the edge so as not to spook the chick over the brim. I settled down against one of the branches with the chick between my legs. Looking down was a very bad idea. I don't suffer from vertigo, but I was feeling a little shaky. The tree, massive though it was, slowly rocked and twisted in the wind. To make things worse, we kept hearing large trees falling over in the forests around us.

Another worry was the chick. It bit my fingers and then Alberto's. It was not being aggressive, it merely thought our fingers were food. At one point it grabbed at my hand with its foot and drew blood with one of its claws. Thankfully it only seemed interested in my hands, especially as it was sitting between my legs.

Scattered around it were the remains of previous meals: skulls of monkeys and sloth fur and claws. The whole nest was like a primate graveyard. Alberto bagged some of these remains to study later.

Below: Formidable talons are driven into the prey's bodies or skulls.

HARPY EAGLE (harpia harpyja)

The harpy eagle is a massive bird with a wingspan of 7ft (2.1m). Males weigh 10–16lb (5–8kg) whilst females are larger at 14–18lb (7–9kg). They live high up in the canopy – up to 120ft (40m) above the ground – of the tropical lowland forests of Central and South America. Mostly they prey on arboreal mammals, from spider monkeys and howling monkeys to anteaters and sloths, but they also take the occasional fawn from the forest floor, and other large birds. The harpy eagle spies on prey from a lookout post in a high tree when hunting, then soars down and uses its feet to capture its quarry and take it back to the nest. The power is in the feet and legs – the harpy eagle has the heaviest, stoutest legs of any bird of prey: lower legs almost the size of an adult human's wrist, toes that span 9in (23cm) and talons up to 5in (12.5cm) long. Females, being larger, are capable of killing prey four times the size of that managed by the males, which weigh the same as them.

2.1m wingspan

habitat

predator: prey size ratio

I was very surprised the adults didn't try and protect their chick from us, but Alberto said they were pretty unflustered about humans in their nests. This was reassuring, as we were in a vulnerable position should they mount an attack. As if to prove this to us, the male returned to the tree with a fresh monkey kill in his talons. He perched on a branch about 30 feet from the nest, looked at us and then calmly flew away with his meal. We decided that it was probably the chick's dinnertime, so we vacated the nest.

Once we were on the ground and were packing away all the ropes, both parents returned to the nest and settled down for a family meal. It was almost arrogant – as if they were so confident in their own power that we couldn't have been a significant threat. Having seen their weapons and what they did to the monkey, I would have to agree.

Opposite: It is very unnerving to sit 150 feet up a tree babysitting a restless harpy chick.
Right: I nearly lost a finger to this hungry mouth.

reticulated python

For strength you need muscle, and a reticulated python is almost nothing but muscle. You could say that about most snakes, but the constrictors use strength to kill and the biggest constrictor is the reticulated python.

You don't find the big ones just anywhere, though. The place to be is Sulawesi, Indonesia. Retics up to 32 feet long have supposedly been found on this island, and caves seems to be a good place to find them.

The cave I found myself dangled over was called 'The Cave of Death', which sounds melodramatic, but when you consider that a 30-foot python can easily take someone my size in a mouthful, it seems quite apt. It is situated about 1.5 miles from the nearest village, and goats and pigs have been known to been eaten by pythons. So something big lives down there.

There is a ladder down into the first part of the cave but, as it was television, it was decided that I should lower myself down on ropes, because it looks more dramatic. This is all very well if you only do it once, but it turned into a sweaty marathon of climbing and lowering, so that the camera could get the best shot.

Once down in the cave I was able to have a little look around. The most striking thing about the entrance was that it was littered with human remains. It looked like a movie set, with bits of skulls, femurs and vertebrae. It was all unmistakably human and very old. One of the locals told us that the cave was an old burial site and indeed there were bits of coffins littered around. It was the first time I had seen anything like this and it gave the place a really hallowed feeling.

Our snake expert, Duncan Macrae, led us deeper into the cave. Duncan is a herpto-culturist, which means he specializes in keeping reptiles. He has always had a passion for snakes but was advised just to keep it as a hobby. After finishing school he travelled to Australia and was making his way back to the UK when he stopped in Indonesia. Duncan got no further. He lives out here and runs his own reptile park and breeding centre.

Duncan checked every nook and cranny for snakes. This is a great area for them as it is so humid and hot. Pretty soon we were totally drenched with sweat and covered with bat droppings. They weren't the only droppings down there, either. Duncan soon found large snake faeces, which were quite fresh. It was becoming more and more likely that we would find our snake.

The cave became thinner and thinner as we moved forward, but then it opened into a larger cavern. Within a few seconds we had sight of our first snake. Duncan had found a python lying on a rock ledge; it was

Opposite: Descending into 'The Cave of Death'. I had to use ropes for visual effect, despite the presence of serviceable ladders.
Below: The entrance to the cave was littered with human remains.

Left: Inside the cave a python is perched on a ledge. It was only about 4 feet long, and so had some growing to do.

only about 4 feet long, so it had a bit of growing to do before it was something like the beast we were after.

Not long after this find we got the snake we wanted. It was coiled up right in the back

RETICULATED PYTHON (python reticulata)

Reticulated pythons are found extensively in Southeast Asia, Indonesia and the Philippines. They are the world's largest snake (the anaconda being the heaviest) – record specimens can be over 30ft (9m), but a more usual size range is 15–20ft (4.6–6.1m). They can weigh 200–250lb (91–113kg). Adult retics are opportunistic feeders capable of overpowering and eating goats, wild boars and even people and have a reputation for a very nasty temperament. The feeding response is largely reflexive and so even if its prey is too big for the python, once it's got a hold it will constrict and kill the victim before realizing its mistake. Snakes are basically one long muscle and this is where the power of the reticulated python lies, as the whole body length can be used to restrain and constrict its prey. Reticulated pythons are found in rainforest and woodland habitats, particularly near streams and rivers. In Sulawesi, where the largest reticulated pythons have been found, visitors are advised not to go walking by streams at dawn and dusk, when pythons may be out hunting. Although people are killed and eaten by these snakes there are no official statistics for the number of human fatalities.

6.1m long

habitat

predator: prey size ratio

of a crevice, but it was a big one. Estimations could only be made from the patterning on its side and the girth of its body, but we guessed that it would be about 11–13 feet long. It was too deep in for us to get a close look and nobody was volunteering to go and get it, so we left it undisturbed.

The cave did go deeper and with the aid of the ropes we dropped down another 50 feet into a huge cavern. It was the size of a cathedral and full of bats. The whole place had a real gothic feel to it, reinforced by an altar-like stone lying right in the centre. The only evidence of serpents was a snake's skeleton lying in this cavern. It was about 10 feet in length and perfectly preserved. It appeared that human remains weren't the only ones down here.

We did have a snake to get a closer look at, though. Duncan had arranged for a python to be caught a few days earlier for us. It was 10 feet long and currently residing in a sack. Deep in the cave, under the illumination of torches, Duncan undid the knots around the neck of the bag and peeled it back. This was fascinating to me, because I had never really seen someone handle a wild snake and I wondered how it would react. Duncan slowly opened the bag, looking for the animal's head, and

take even longer. Large boars or deer can take up to twelve hours to kill and eat.

By the time we had finished filming I was completely shattered. It was time for me to let it go. Actually it was more of a mutual agreement. Duncan peeled the body off me and, after a count of three, we released the snake onto the ground. It immediately struck out at us and as we leapt backwards we bowled Simon over, who was filming behind us. Without it crushing the wind out of me, I could really get a good look at the python. They are such beautiful and graceful creatures. It was nice to be able to let this one go back where it belonged and hopefully one day it will live to be a truly massive specimen.

Really big snakes are not popular in Sulawesi. They are seen as a threat to livestock and humans. We saw a 20-foot specimen that had been caught and killed. It had recently eaten a large meal and the bulge in its belly was enormous. It was such a shame to see such a beautiful animal killed through fear, but I might have felt different if the bulge contained my goat, or even my child. Thankfully, its last meal had been wild boar.

Above and right: The tragic death of an amazing animal. The bulge in its stomach is a whole wild boar.

very gently took hold of the neck just behind it. He could then carefully remove the snake from the bag. At this point the snake started to move. It twisted and turned, trying to lash its body onto anything. I picked up its back end and it immediately lashed itself around me, releasing a stream of faeces all up my arm. When snakes feel threatened they often void themselves as a defence mechanism.

Duncan then passed me the head. It took only the lightest touch to restrain the head, but the body was beginning to give me a bit of a squeeze. It had hooked a loop of body over my right shoulder and another down around my waist. When it contracted it felt like I was suddenly carrying something ten times the weight. It could push, pull, bend and twist in just about every direction with minor changes in position. Just when I sussed out what one part of it was doing, another part would suddenly squeeze me elsewhere. I could easily imagine what it must feel like to be squeezed to death by this thing's big brother. The worst part would be that every time you breathed out it would tighten its grip, allowing you less and less air until you suffocated. With large prey this can take a long time and eating it afterwards can

polar bear

Svalbard is a scrap of land way up north in the High Arctic. It has one town and a good population of polar bears. Filming polar bears in the wild is fraught with danger, due to both the bears themselves and the conditions. Luckily, we had a couple of guys on the ground already. Doug Allen is a wildlife cameraman with a great deal of experience in polar filming and Jason Roberts is an Australian who now lives on Svalbard, where he works as a fixer.

Jason specializes in Arctic and Antarctic productions and had hired all our external clothing, including hats, balaclavas, snow

Left: More than adequate protection, with a flare gun and a .44 Magnum.

suits, mittens, hats and goggles. By the time we got all the gear on, we could hardly move.

Doug had been filming the bears here for the BBC for three weeks already and had a good idea of where we could get good shots of the bears. The east side of the island was our best bet, but that involved us travelling on snowmobiles. Jason had arranged the snowmobile hire and we spent an afternoon getting used to driving them.

Our base camp was in a tiny hunter's cabin on the east side of the island. We had to set tripwires and flares around the equipment outside to protect the gear from bear attack. More worryingly, there were patches in the cabin walls where bears had broken in. This is quite common out here and bullet holes in the door showed that it wasn't always when they were empty.

Finding bears didn't prove too difficult, it just took quite a long time. We headed out onto the pack ice in the snowmobiles and kept looking. The pack ice was like another planet. I had expected it to be flat, but it was creased up into large ridges that we had to weave through carefully. When we stopped the engines the air was totally silent. There was no sign of life anywhere. It was weird to think that there was enough food here to feed one of the largest land predators.

We occasionally came across icebergs caught in the pack ice. They were an iridescent blue, a stark contrast to the surrounding whiteness, looked more like glass than ice and, amazingly, didn't feel that cold to

touch. This was because they were too cold to melt and cover my hand with ice water. Jason and Doug climbed up the icebergs to scan the rest of the ice for bears.

After a number of hours we were ready for a break and some food. Director and producer Marielle Wyse was also getting very cold. The main reason for this was because she had to strip off her suit every time she needed to pee. It didn't help that she had accidentally peed into the hood of her suit. We were near another cabin and we headed that way so that we could get her warmed up. When we reached the cabin I soon warmed up, because I had to dig the door out. It was buried under 6 feet of snow and it took me about half an hour with a shovel before we could get inside.

After a warm drink and a few pieces of chocolate we were ready to go out once more. Pretty much immediately we were blessed with bears. We spotted a lone bear walking from the shore over the ice to the open water. It was about 350 yards from us when it settled down to rest on the snow. I am amazed how comfortable polar bears are in this environment.

We moved in as close as we could on the snowmobiles. Every so often the bear would stand up and take a look at us. Twice it stood right up on its back legs looking almost comical, like an embarrassed child waiting to see the headmaster.

Doug was worried about scaring it off with the snowmobiles, so we stopped about 180 yards away and moved in on foot. Jason stayed behind with the snowmobiles in case we need assistance quickly. I was given the

Above: This bear had been tagged and numbered by research scientists.
Opposite: Huge icebergs punctured the pack ice.

The icebergs were
an iridescent
blue, a stark
contrast to the
surrounding
whiteness

flare gun and carried Doug's tripod and Jake and Simon followed behind us. When we got sufficiently near Doug set up his camera. Then we crept even closer. Jason said we looked like a cartoon from his vantage point. We all tiptoed forward in a line until the bear looked up and we froze to the spot. When it dropped its head we continued forward. I was holding the flare gun in readiness, because I wasn't as confident as Doug seemed to be about the bear's patience.

We set up about 40 yards away and started filming. The bear lay sprawled on the snow looking quite relaxed. Occasionally it would look up and yawn or glance in our direction. We stayed there for about fifteen minutes talking and filming and it didn't bat an eyelid. It was completely unmoved by our presence.

Finally it got up from its rest and walked slowly past us. Jason was concerned that it was too close and so started his snowmobile and came to meet us, whereupon the bear changed course and moved away from us. Doug said that it was good to see a bear so relaxed during filming and that it proved to him that he had got it right when he saw them walk away unfazed by their encounter. I agreed wholeheartedly. The veterinary work I am usually involved in necessitates interference with animals, so it was a very special experience for me to play the part of a mere observer.

I paced out the distance we had been from the bear – it was 100 feet. That is about as close as Doug likes to get to them, so we were very lucky indeed. Where it had

Opposite: The polar bear's strength lies in its heavy body, particularly in its forelegs and huge paws.
Below: A polar bear can smell a seal lair and smash down through its roof in seconds.

POLAR BEAR (ursus maritimus)

The polar bear is the world's largest carnivore, weighing in at around 1,323lb (600kg). Its great strength lies in its heavy body, particularly the massive forelegs, which are topped by dinner-plate-sized paws. The bear uses these to smash through the sea ice to seal dens below or to flip large seals and beluga whales out of the water. The polar bear can sniff out a seal den from over half a mile (1km) away. Standing on its hind legs and pounding down on the wind-packed ice using its massive forelegs, it breaks through and feeds at leisure on the seal pups below. The bear feeds almost exclusively on marine mammals but is an opportunistic hunter and has taken humans. Polar bears live in all of the polar regions of the northern hemisphere, and are found largely on the sea ice that forms on the edges of the land where the northern seas meets the shore; their Latin name, *Ursus maritimus*, actually means 'sea bear'. They are good swimmers and are most at home hunting on the ice following the areas of temporary water also favoured by their prey. Polar bears can live for up to twenty-five years and grow to a height of 8.2–9.8ft (2.5–3m).

3m tall

habitat

predator: prey size ratio

been sleeping there was a seal lair. Ring seals break through patches of thin ice under the snow and burrow out lairs to give birth to their young in. The bears can smell through the snow and smash down through the roof of the lair to try and catch the seals. There was no evidence of a kill here, so this time the seals had escaped. The hole in the roof was about 3 feet deep and Doug demonstrated how hard the snow was by jumping up and down adjacent to the hole. He made no impression in the hard packed snow, and yet a bear could break through this depth of snow in a matter of a few seconds. Even with the shovel it would have taken me a good fifteen minutes to create such a hole.

Doug suggested I take a look in the hole, so I plunged head-first down it and quickly became lodged there. The others took the opportunity to ram me further in until I was totally stuck. I couldn't help thinking I was going to come face to face

We continued travelling north to find more bears and had been going for quite some time when Doug stopped us and we had a discussion as to whether we should stay out or return. We had already been up for nearly twenty hours and we were still two hours from base. Jason was keen to keep going, but he was in a minority of one. That was until he spotted a mother and two of this year's cubs on the horizon. We just had to have a closer look. Unfortunately, the mother was very wary, so I had to be satisfied with watching her family through the binoculars. The cubs were gorgeous. They stumbled along behind the long, ambling gait of their mother, occasionally stopping and looking curiously in our direction.

Jason then spotted their last meal. We went to check it out. The whole area looked like a scene from *Psycho*. Blood was everywhere. There was a crater in the snow sprayed pink where the mother had caught an adult ring seal and running from this was a dark red trail leading to its grisly carcass. Surprisingly, all the meat on the seal was left untouched. For polar bears, the favoured part of the ring seals is the blubber and skin, and this had been completely devoured. The head had been almost turned inside out and was nearly unrecognisable. If I'd had any doubts as to the strength of polar bears, they were gone now.

As we turned to leave, Jason gave me his binoculars to have a look at the vicious predator, as she had stopped about half a mile away. She was sitting down on the snow cradling her cubs as she allowed them to suckle. The transition from extreme violence to an act of utter gentleness was strangely hypnotic.

As we returned to the cabin I was left thinking of Doug's comment that we would leave this harsh wilderness behind, yet the bears would continue to live and thrive out here. It was a good feeling.

Opposite: Polar bears are most at home on the ice following areas of water favoured by their prey.
Above: The remains of a seal killing. When the polar bear gets it right the results are gruesome.

with an angry seal. After I was exhausted, Doug had a look himself and it would have been rude not to return the favour of cramming him in. It was a surreal moment, standing there in the vast whiteness with a pair of short legs waggling about in the air and muffled Scottish cursing coming from under the snow.

killer whale

ULTIMATE KILLER

Seeing killer whales (or orcas) is hard enough, never mind filming them. Even though they are the most widespread mammal on the planet, except for humans, they still prove to be pretty elusive. Broadly speaking there are two types of orca – the transients that move around a lot and eat marine mammals, and the residents that live year-round in one area and eat fish. They both belong to the same species, but behave very differently.

Our best chance to see orcas came in the form of the residents that live off the coast of British Columbia, Canada. There is a healthy population of residents and transients in the area, as well as the know-how to find them.

We had sensibly enlisted the help of Jim Borrowman, who runs whale-watching tours, and Larry Roy, who runs kayaking trips. The idea was to take Jim's boat to where the whales were and launch Larry and me in the kayaks. All we needed was the whales.

The problem was, there weren't any. For the first time on record, all the orcas had super-podded, which means that all the individual whale pods came together as one, and over 100 of them moved way down the coast. Nobody knows why.

There is a huge network of whale watchers that passes on information regarding the whales' whereabouts. Their resources even stretch to underwater microphones placed strategically in the area to listen for them passing.

Despite no news of the whales' position, Jim persuaded us to head out onto the water on a hunch he had. He has been fol-lowing the orcas for so many years now that we would have been foolish to doubt him.

Jim has seen how powerful these animals really are. The transients that eat marine mammals have to stun their prey quickly to stop them escaping or defending them-selves. Jim has seen orcas butting bull seals out of the water, breaching out of the waves to crash down onto prey and, with a flick of their powerful tails, sending fully grown porpoises sailing through the air. They have even been filmed taking on a blue whale, which is the largest animal on the planet. Even the fish-eating residents show amazing power. They have been recorded moving their tails so hard underwater that the shock-wave stuns shoals of herring.

We travelled for about three hours until Jim stopped the boat and pointed forward. Large black fins were just visible in the dis-tance coming towards us. We waited for them to approach and pretty soon we could make out the black-and-white bodies break-ing through the surface, releasing a jet of air and water. Jim pointed out the head of the pod, which was a female recorded as being born in 1946. With her were her off-spring and further generations. Male orcas stay with their mothers all their life and there was one adult male with this pod. The males have much larger dorsal fins and reach greater weights, up to 9 tons.

The pod was moving along the shoreline quite steadily, occasionally foraging for food. It was difficult to know exactly where they were as they took about three breaths in succession and then submerged for min-utes at a time. The longest submerged time

Opposite: Killer whales are massive animals, weighing up to 9 tons.

Jim has witnessed was fourteen minutes. The whales seemed indifferent to our presence and even actively approached the boat. At one point a mother and calf surfaced adjacent to the boat and we could see right down their blowholes.

It was time to try the kayaks. Larry had given me some coaching earlier and I felt fairly confident despite a previous accident. I had been paddling past Simon, who was filming me from Jim's boat, and I got a little too close. I smacked into the camera, nearly displacing it and Simon into the water. Unfortunately I wasn't as lucky and

Above: The orcas were all around us, and we had to paddle hard to match their pace.
Below: Male killer whales have much larger dorsal fins than the females.
Opposite: This resident whale will cruise for miles looking for fish.

promptly capsized. The water here is fairly cold, but I was on the boat pretty quickly and, after a brief striptease in front of the camera, was back in dry clothes again.

Larry has been running kayaking tours here for seventeen years and he was the perfect coach. The whales were still moving up the shore in our direction and he got us into the perfect position to let them meet us. He told me that the whales will approach certain people, especially pregnant women, and won't approach others. I was afraid we were going to be the latter, but he assured me the whales liked him. I could understand why.

I could hear the orcas breathing behind me as they surfaced, but I couldn't turn round. The next thing I knew they were all around us, surfacing to the left and right, and even between us. I had to paddle hard to match their pace, even though they were only cruising. It was an utterly magical experience. I know people get very sentimental around whales and dolphins, but there is something very special about a wild animal that chooses to spend time with you, even if it is just out of curiosity.